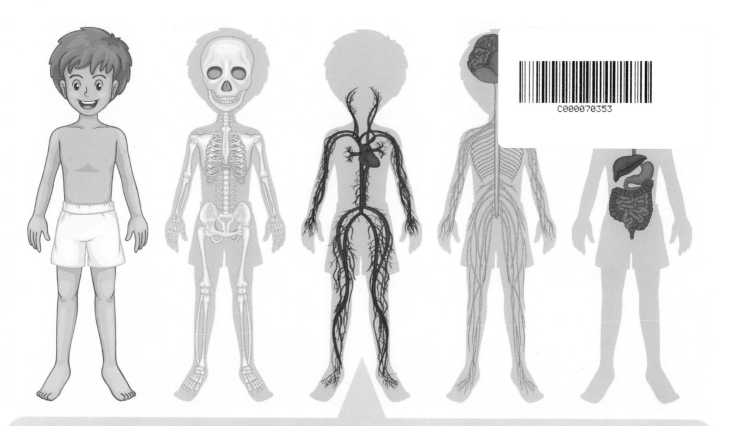

C000070353

A "system" is a set of organs that work together to provide a common function. There are 10 major systems in the human body:

−The skeletal system, consisting of bones, cartilage, tendons and ligaments.

−The muscular system is responsible for movement.

−The circulatory system is responsible for the transport of nutrients, gases (oxygen, carbon dioxide).

−The nervous system, which includes the brain, spinal cord and peripheral nerves.

−The respiratory system (nose, trachea, lungs) is an interface for the exchange of gases between the blood and the environment.

−The digestive system is responsible for breaking down, breaking down and absorbing nutrients.

−The role of the urinary system (kidney, ureter, bladder, urethra) is to filter and eliminate cellular waste.

−The endocrine system is made up of the many glands that secrete hormones (e.g. pituitary, thyroid, pancreas, adrenals).

−reproductive system differs between the sexes. In women, it includes the ovaries, fallopian tubes, uterus, vagina and mammary glands; in men, the testicles, bladder glands and penis.

−The lymphatic system (lymph, lymphatic vessels, lymph nodes) has the main purpose of destroying and eliminating microbes.

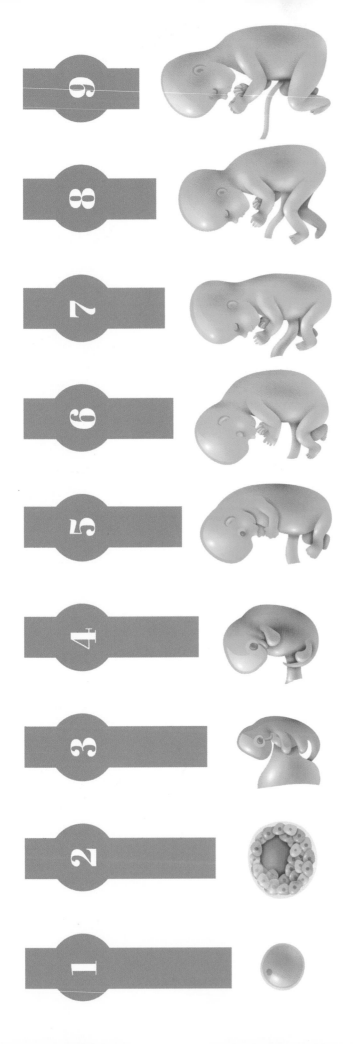

During the long stages of pregnancy, the fetus develops rapidly, from fertilization to a full baby. The fetus is the product of reproduction, starting in the third month of pregnancy. Before this period, it is an embryo. The foetal period is characterized by rapid growth: if at eight weeks, the foetus weighs around one gram, it will give birth to a baby weighing 2.7 and 4.1 kg.

During the third and fourth months: the body lengthens, the brain grows, the face takes on a human appearance.

During the fifth month, the foetus adopts the foetal position because of the lack of space and the mother feels her first movements.

During the sixth and seventh months: the weight increases significantly, the eyes open.

During the eighth and ninth months, the skin takes on a pinkish-white colour and the foetus continues to grow before a few days of delivery.

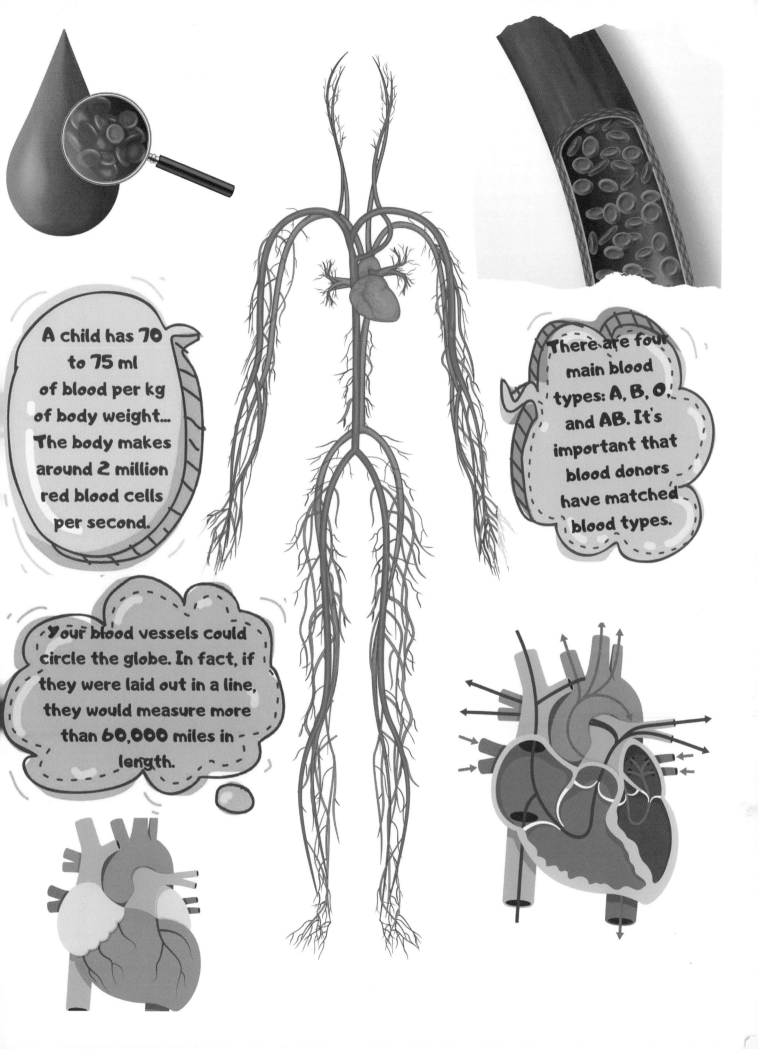

ANALYSIS FOR PREGNANCY

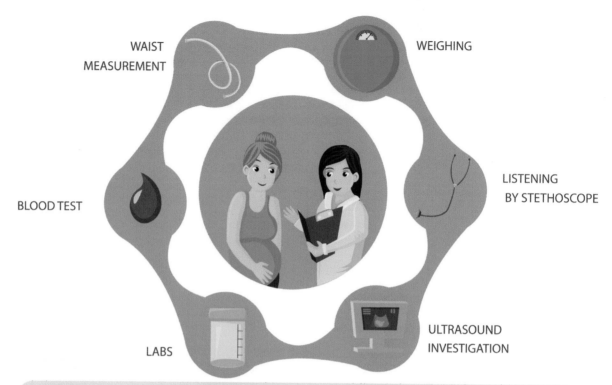

When your mother was pregnant with you, she regularly visits the gynaecologist for blood tests, Ultrasound every trimester for a good evolution of the pregnancy.

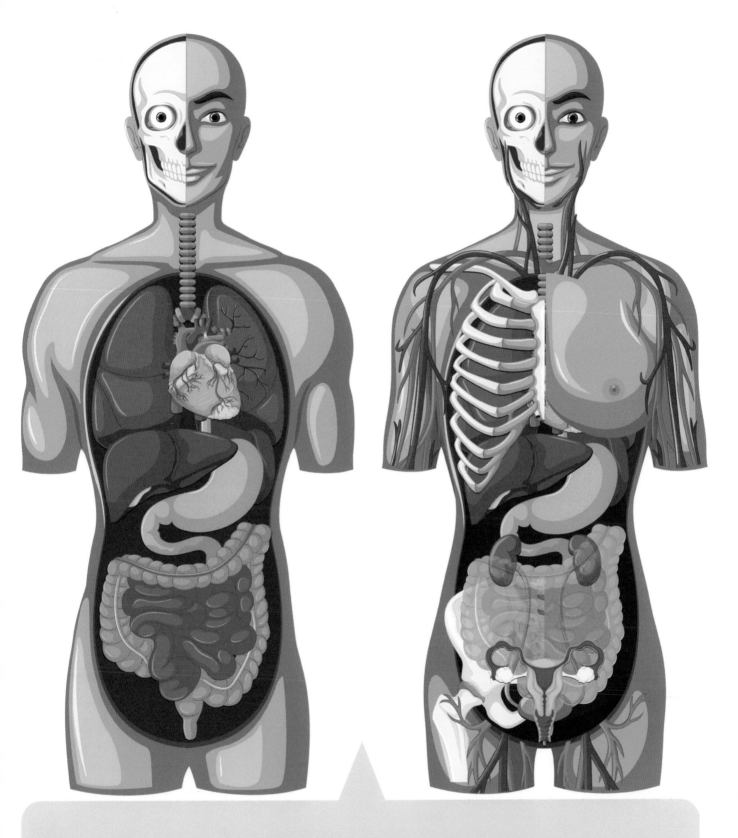

The human body consists of several superficial and internal layers, starting with the skin, then the muscles, organs, Each layer has a special role .... try to identify these layers and organs in this picture.

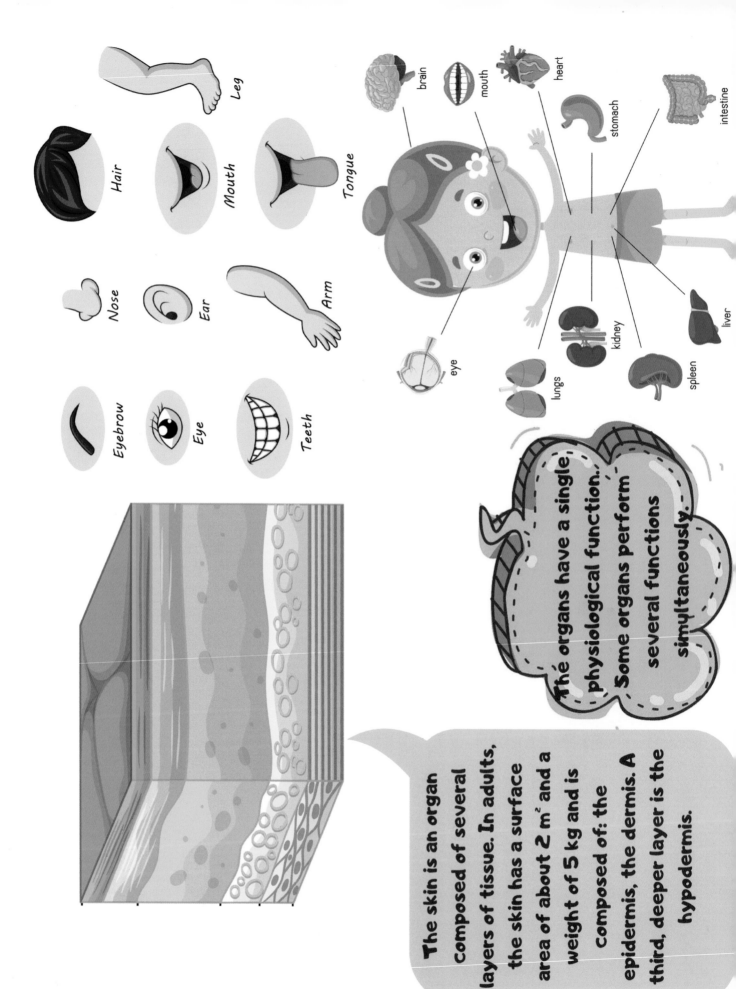

Leg

Hair

Mouth

Tongue

Nose

Ear

Arm

Eyebrow

Eye

Teeth

brain

mouth

heart

stomach

intestine

eye

kidney

liver

lungs

spleen

The organs have a single physiological function. Some organs perform several functions simultaneously.

The skin is an organ composed of several layers of tissue. In adults, the skin has a surface area of about 2 m² and a weight of 5 kg and is composed of: the epidermis, the dermis. A third, deeper layer is the hypodermis.

THE HUMAN BODY
INTERNAL ORGANS

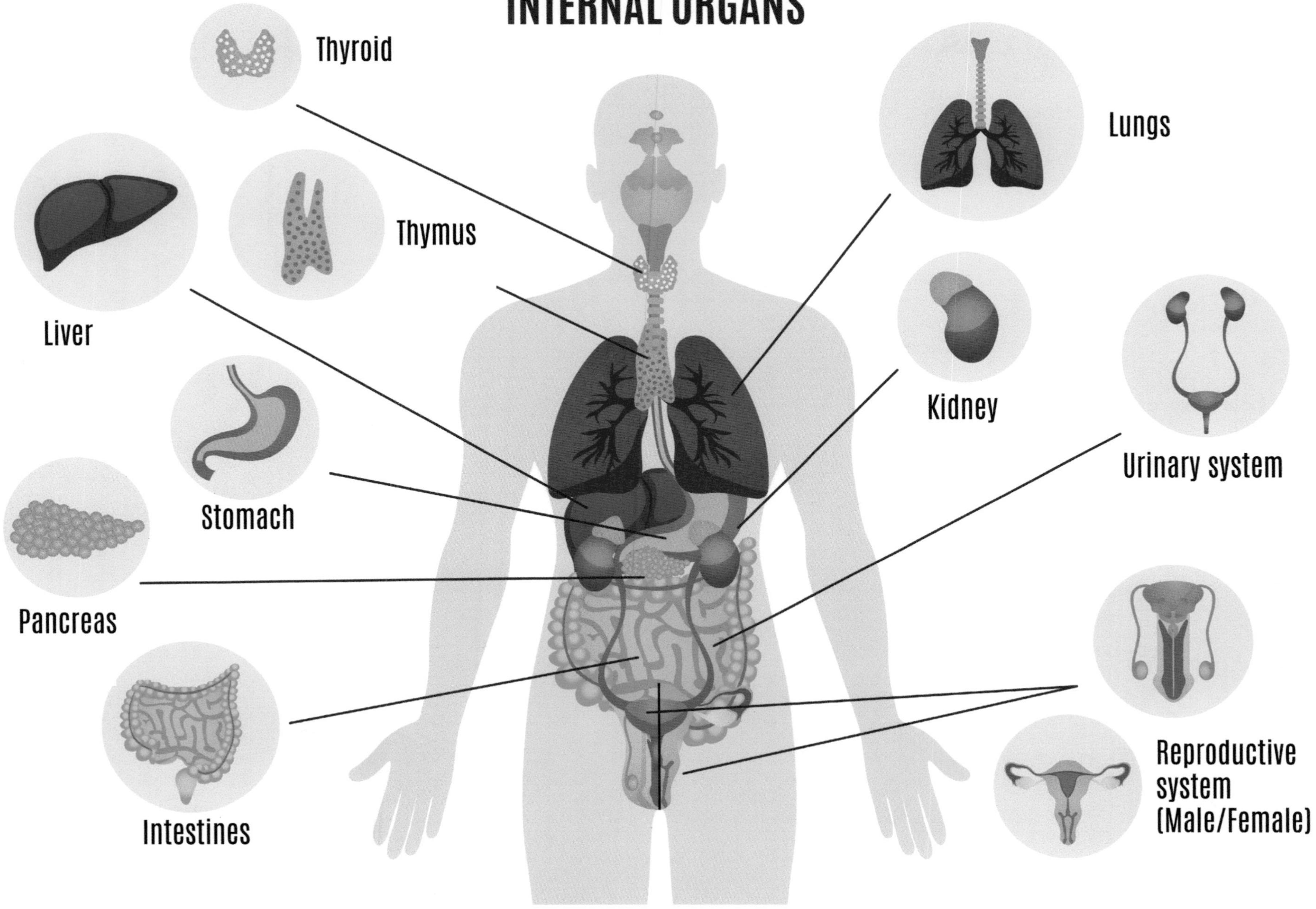

Lungs

Urinary system

Reproductive system (Male/Female)

Kidney

Thyroid

Thymus

Liver

Stomach

Pancreas

Intestines

Cells of The Human Body

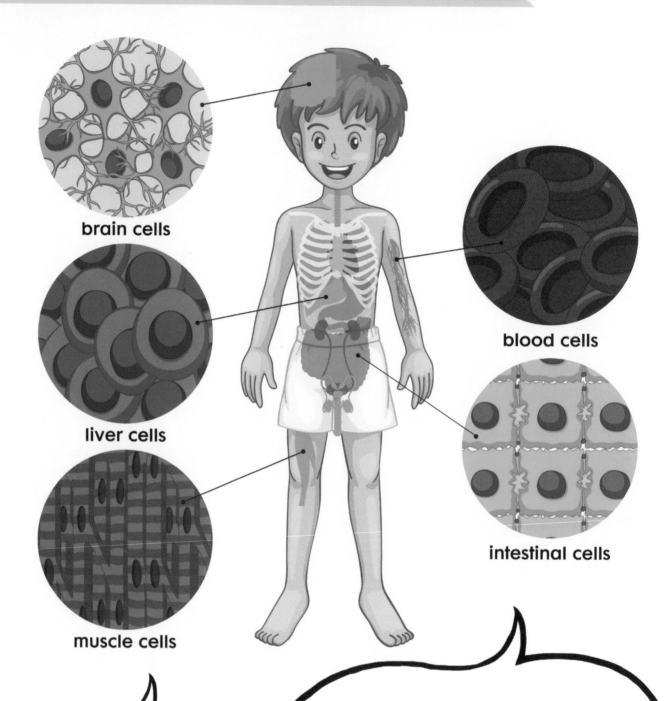

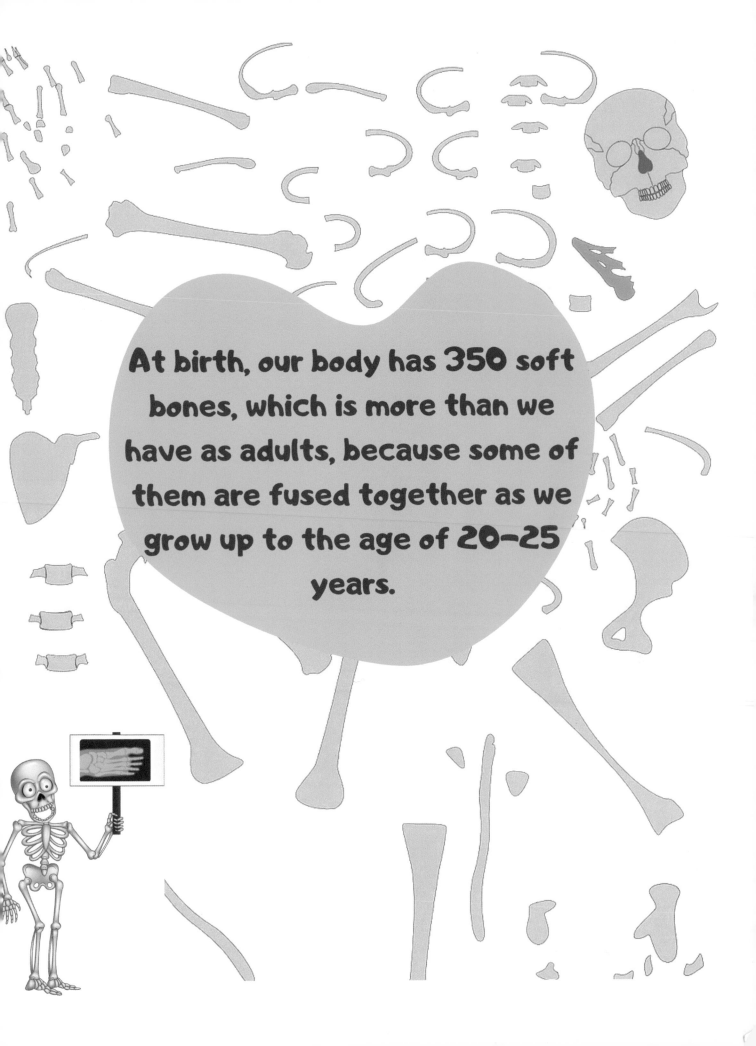

At birth, our body has **350** soft bones, which is more than we have as adults, because some of them are fused together as we grow up to the age of **20-25** years.

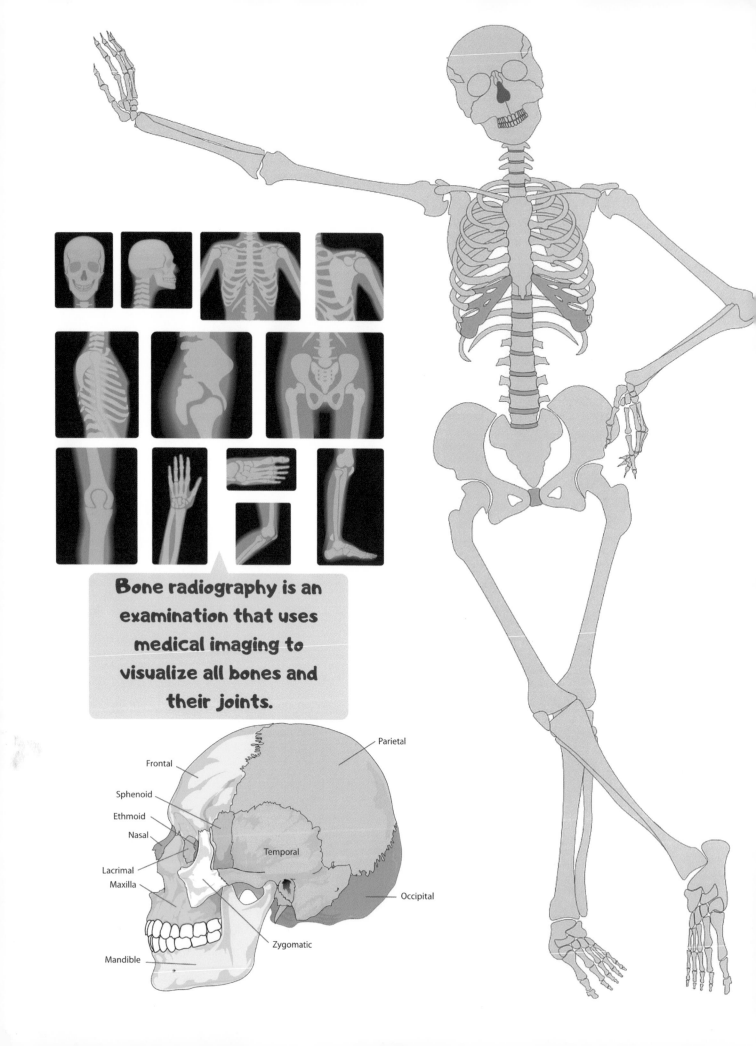

Bone radiography is an examination that uses medical imaging to visualize all bones and their joints.

Frontal
Parietal
Sphenoid
Ethmoid
Nasal
Temporal
Lacrimal
Maxilla
Occipital
Zygomatic
Mandible

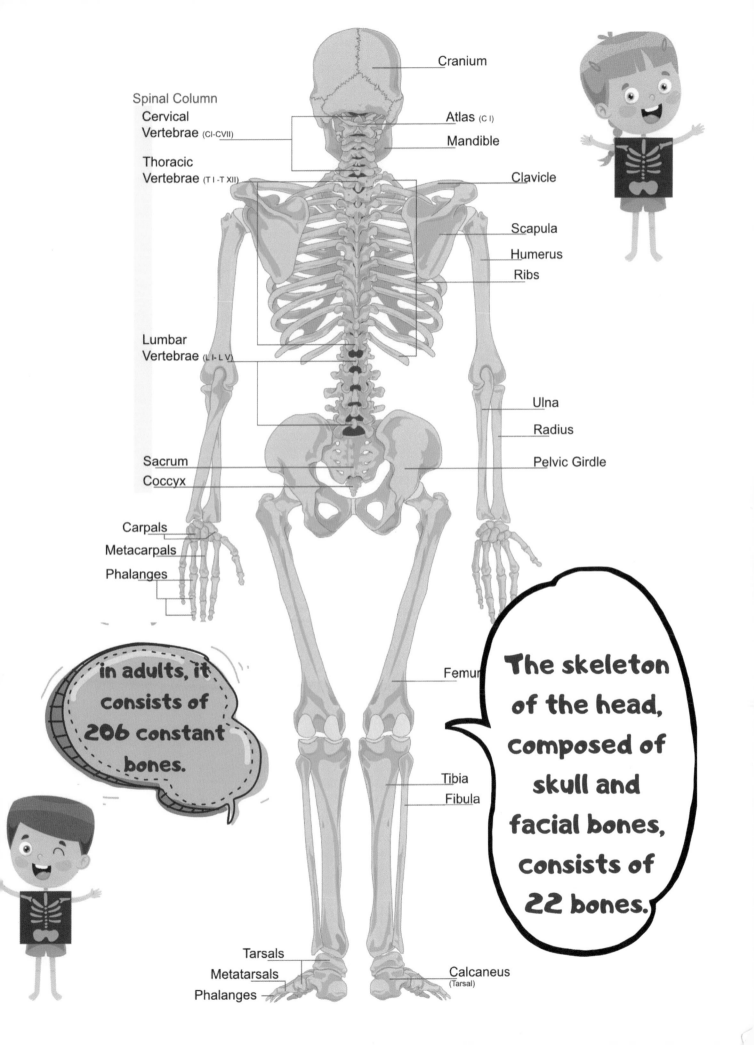

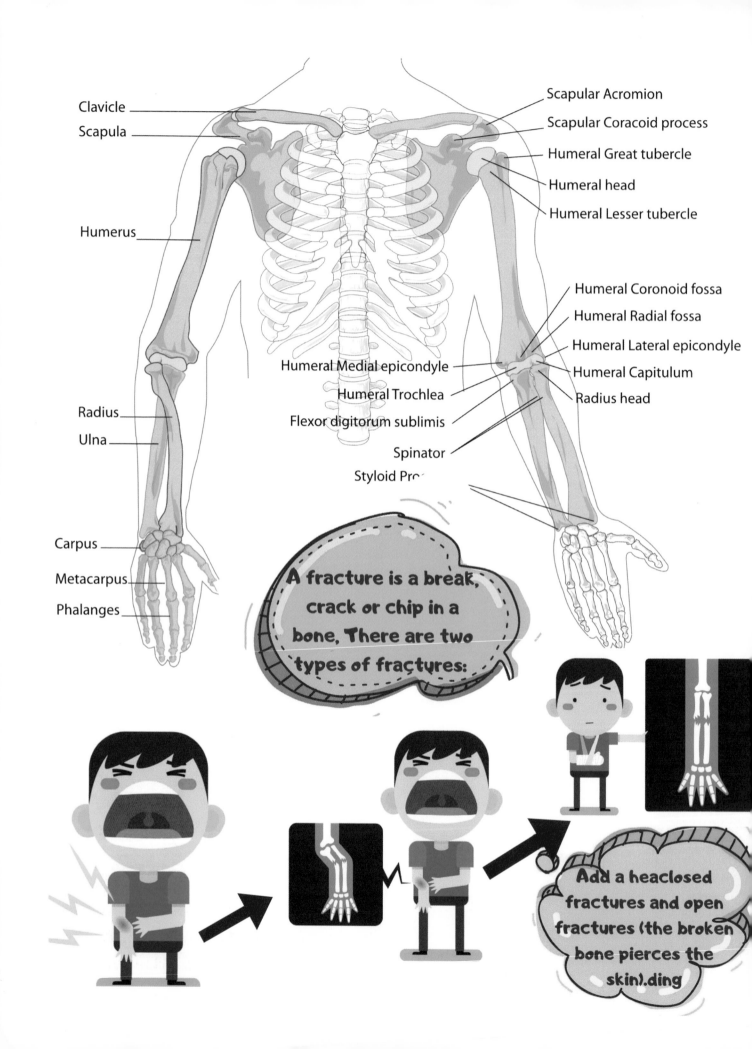

UPPER TEETH

PREMOLARS   CANINES   INCISORS   CANINES   PREMOLARS

LOWER TEETH

The first teeth to grow are the incisors. Those of the lower jaw appear between the ages of 6 and 10 months, and those of the upper jaw, between 7 and 12 months, a person will generally have 20 primary teeth and then 32 permanent teeth.

Tasting is the sense that allows the identification of chemical substances in the form of solutions by means of chemoreceptors located on the tongue.

| UMAMI | SOUR | SWEET | BITTER | SALTY |

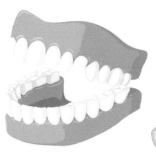
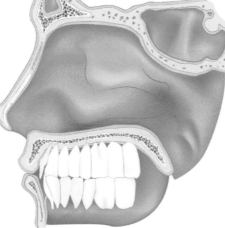

Brush your teeth after every meal, or at least twice a day, including brushing before going to bed. A diet that is too rich in starch and sugar leads to the build-up of plaque and the production of acids that cause tooth decay

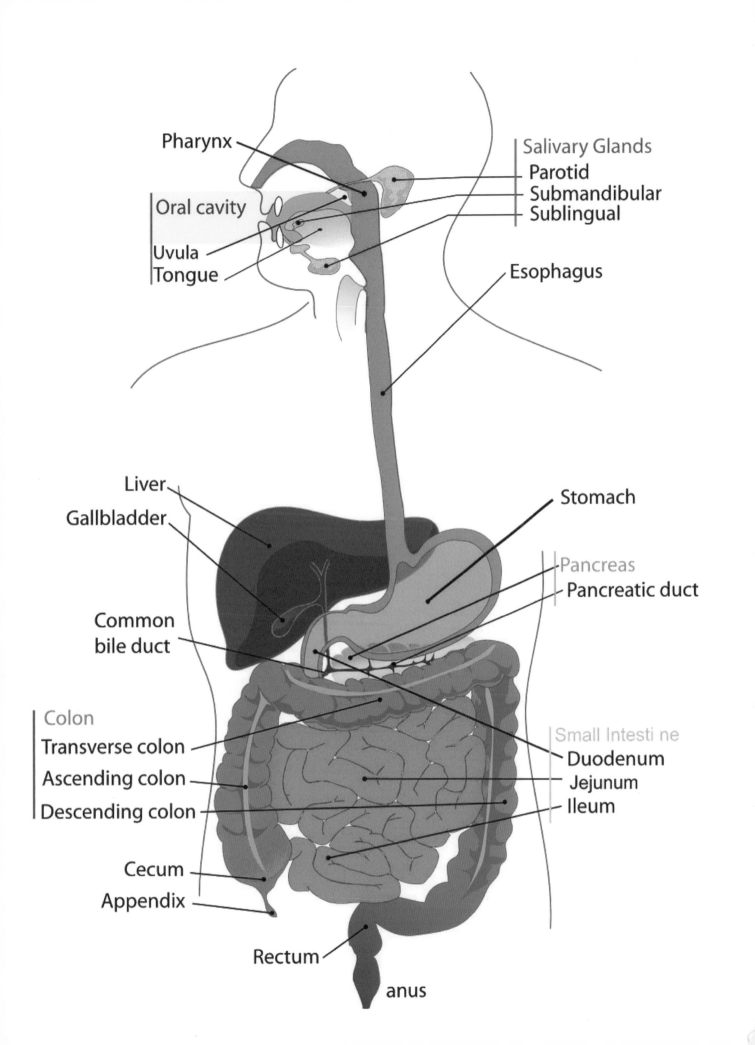

Pharynx

Salivary Glands
Parotid
Submandibular
Sublingual

Oral cavity

Uvula
Tongue

Esophagus

Liver

Stomach

Gallbladder

Pancreas
Pancreatic duct

Common
bile duct

Colon
Transverse colon

Small Intesti ne
Duodenum

Ascending colon

Jejunum

Descending colon

Ileum

Cecum

Appendix

Rectum

anus

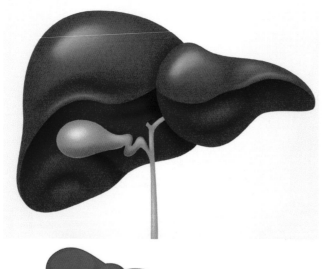

The liver is a unique abdominal organ, housed in humans on the right side of the abdomen. The liver has three vital functions: a purification function, a synthesis function and a storage function.

. . . .

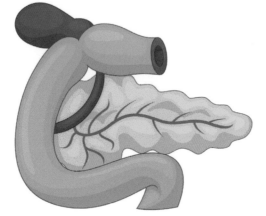

The pancreas produces, on the one hand, pancreatic juice, a secretion rich in bicarbonates and enzymes poured into the duodenum and which take part in digestion, and, on the other hand, hormones poured into the blood, with various functions: glucagon, insulin...

. . . .

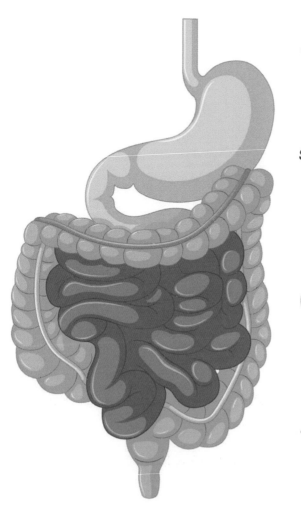

The stomach receives the food chewed in the mouth and swallowed into the oesophagus. In humans, the stomach is shaped like a capital J, in adulthood it is 15 cm high, contains 0.5 l when empty, and can hold up to 4 litres.

. . . .

The small intestine is the part of the human digestive tract located between the stomach and the large intestine (colon). The small intestine is the main place where nutrients are absorbed by the body: it grows in length to provide a maximum absorption surface, its average length is 6 m.

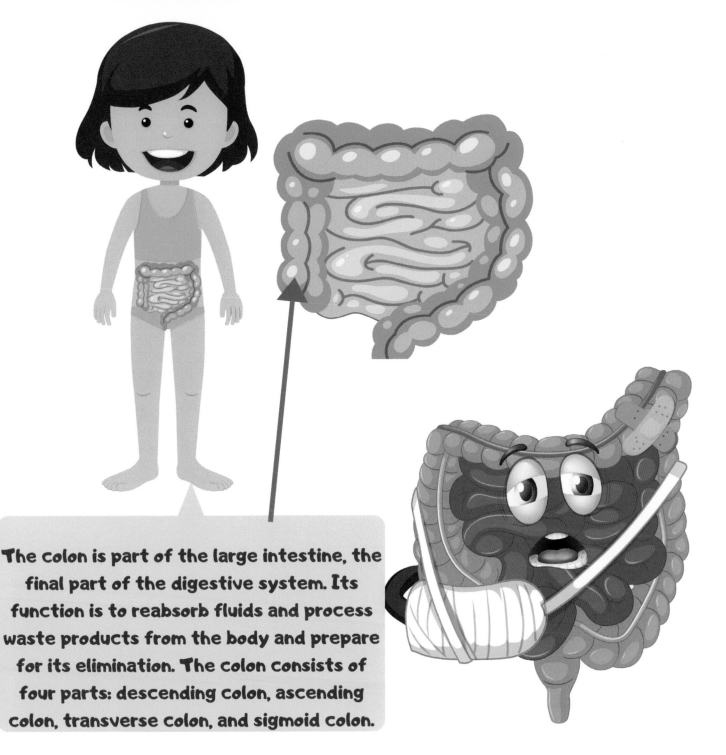

The colon is part of the large intestine, the final part of the digestive system. Its function is to reabsorb fluids and process waste products from the body and prepare for its elimination. The colon consists of four parts: descending colon, ascending colon, transverse colon, and sigmoid colon.

Gastroenteritis is an inflammation of the digestive system that can lead to nausea, vomiting, abdominal cramps, flatulence and diarrhea, as well as dehydration, fever and headache. Gastroenteritis can be bacterial or viral in origin due to the consumption of contaminated food or water.
Prevention: Hand and surface hygiene.

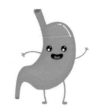

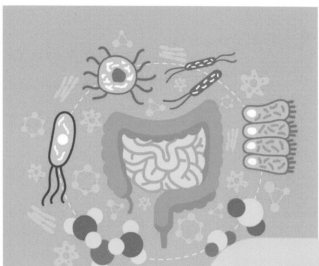

A good diet provides the body with essential nutrients: fluid, essential amino acids, protein2, fatty acids, vitamins, minerals, and enough calories.

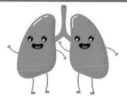

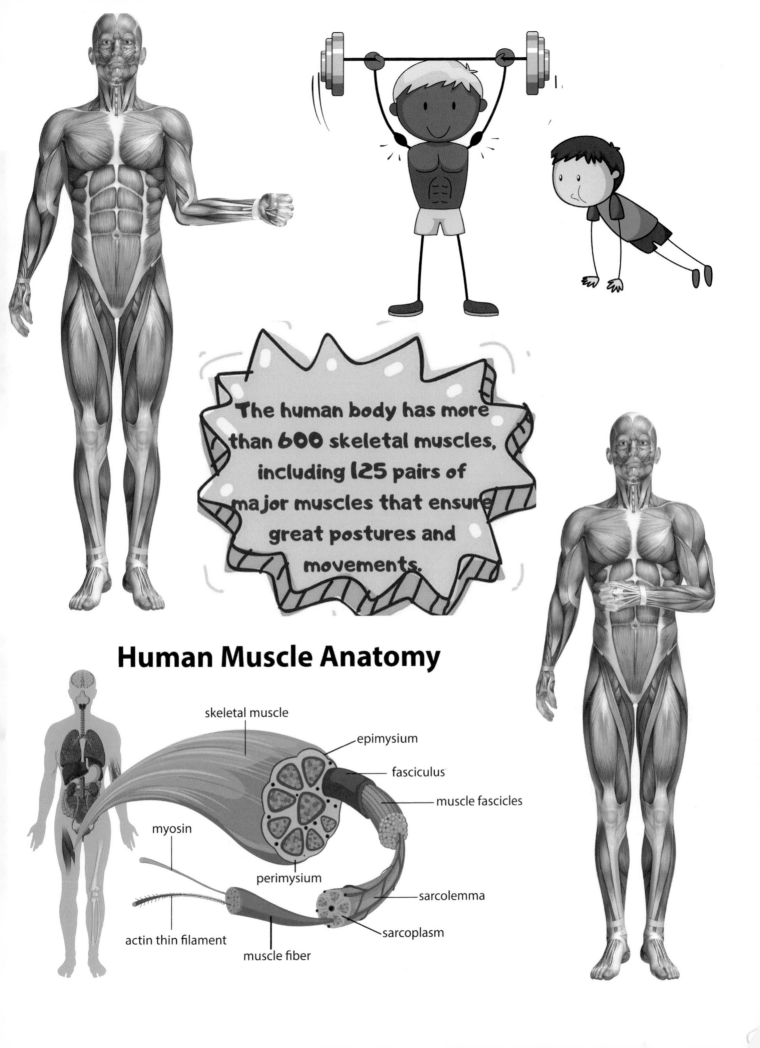

The human body has more than 600 skeletal muscles, including 125 pairs of major muscles that ensure great postures and movements.

Human Muscle Anatomy

skeletal muscle

epimysium

fasciculus

muscle fascicles

myosin

perimysium

sarcolemma

actin thin filament

sarcoplasm

muscle fiber

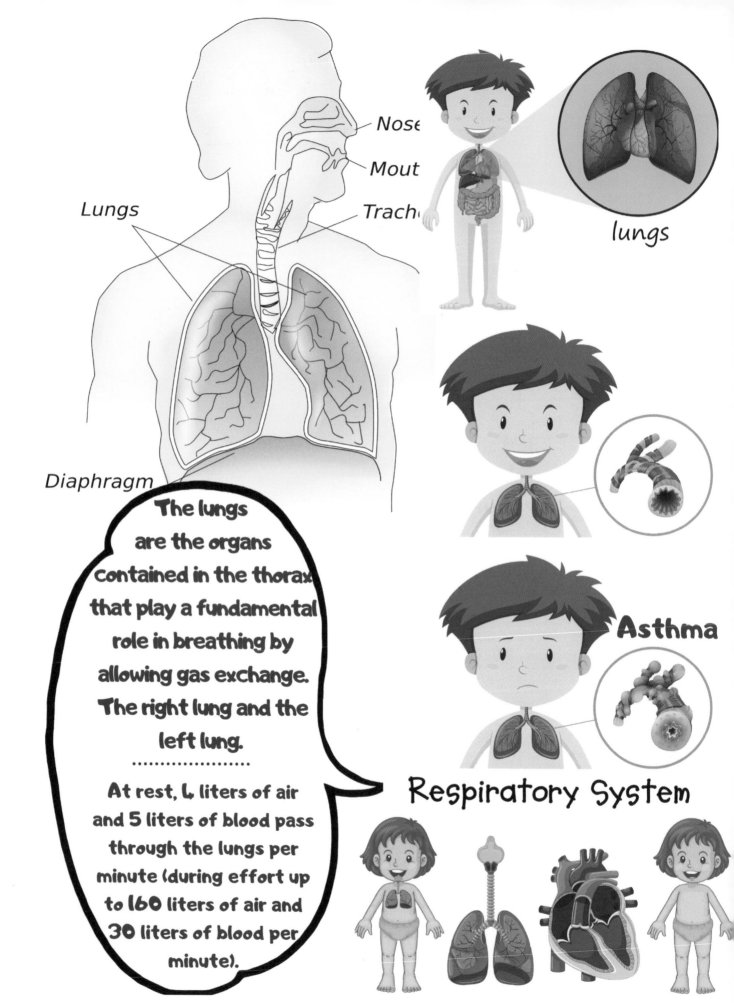

Nose

Mout[h]

Trach[ea]

Lungs

Diaphragm

lungs

Asthma

Respiratory System

The lungs are the organs contained in the thorax that play a fundamental role in breathing by allowing gas exchange. The right lung and the left lung.

·····················

At rest, 4 liters of air and 5 liters of blood pass through the lungs per minute (during effort up to 160 liters of air and 30 liters of blood per minute).

Nervous System

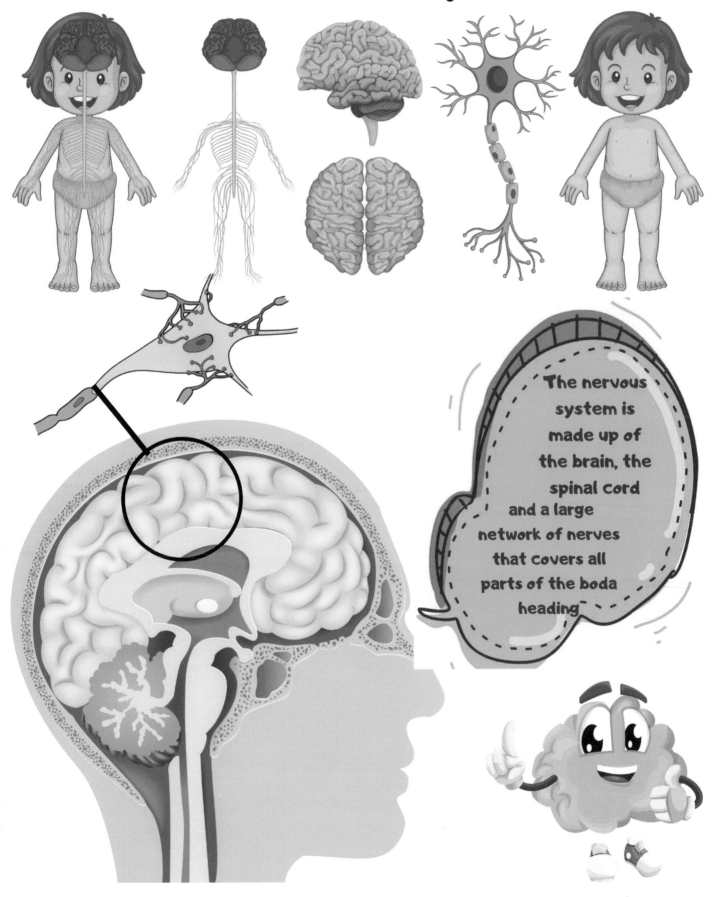

The nervous system is made up of the brain, the spinal cord and a large network of nerves that covers all parts of the boda heading

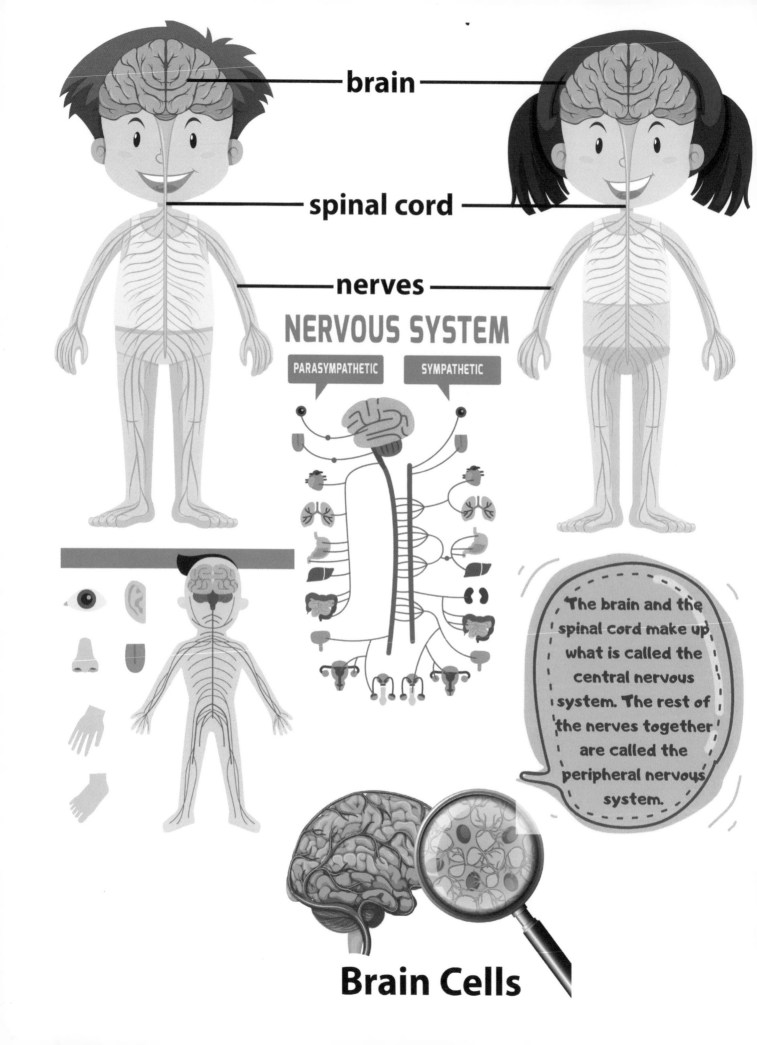

brain

spinal cord

nerves

NERVOUS SYSTEM

PARASYMPATHETIC   SYMPATHETIC

The brain and the spinal cord make up what is called the central nervous system. The rest of the nerves together are called the peripheral nervous system.

Brain Cells

Blood Flow of the Human Heart

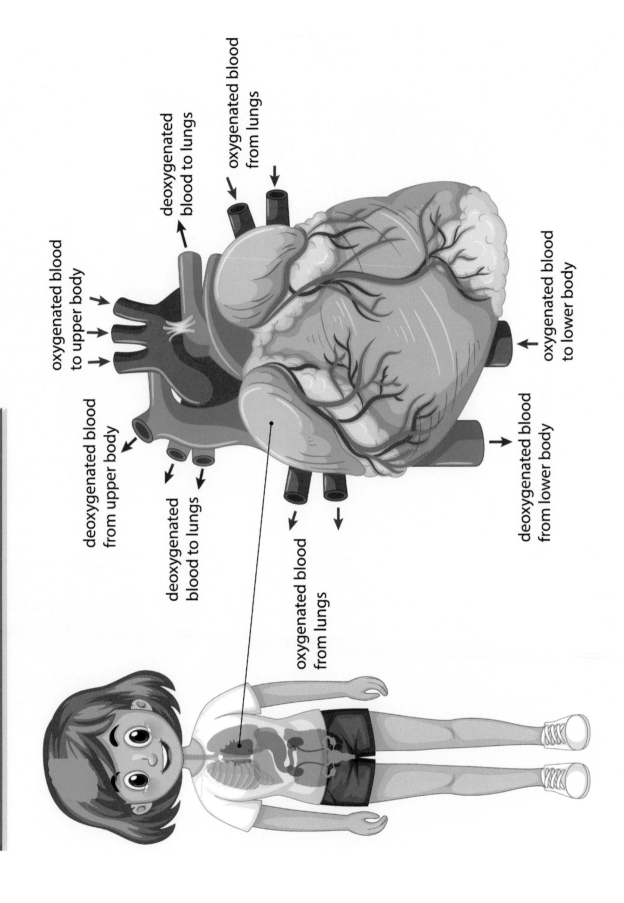

deoxygenated blood to lungs

oxygenated blood from lungs

oxygenated blood to upper body

oxygenated blood to lower body

deoxygenated blood from upper body

deoxygenated blood to lungs

deoxygenated blood from lower body

oxygenated blood from lungs

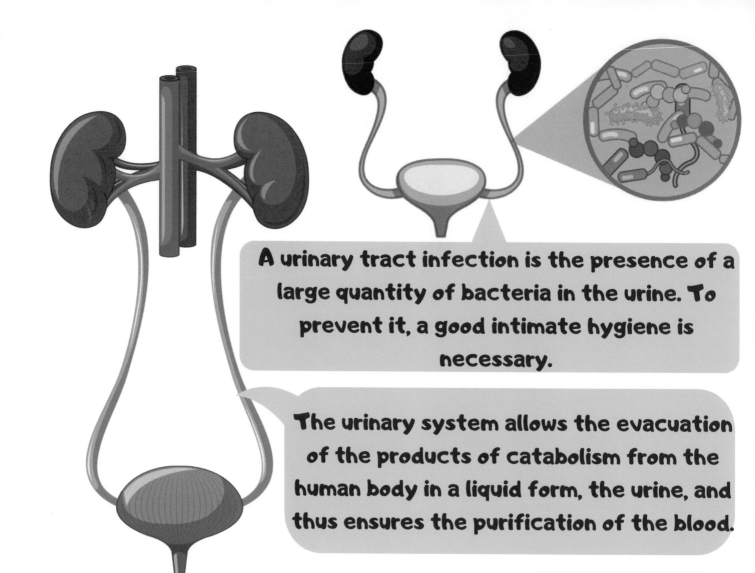

A urinary tract infection is the presence of a large quantity of bacteria in the urine. To prevent it, a good intimate hygiene is necessary.

The urinary system allows the evacuation of the products of catabolism from the human body in a liquid form, the urine, and thus ensures the purification of the blood.

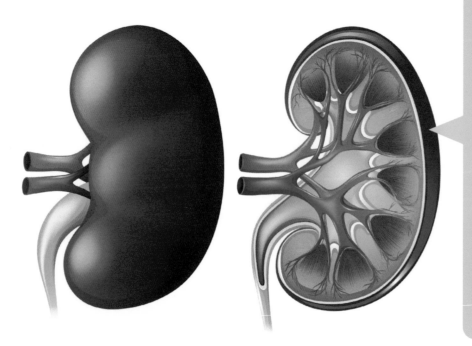

The urinary tract consists of the kidneys, ureters, bladder, urethra and urinary meatus. Every day, a human being produces 0.8 to 2 litres of urine.

Anatomy illustration

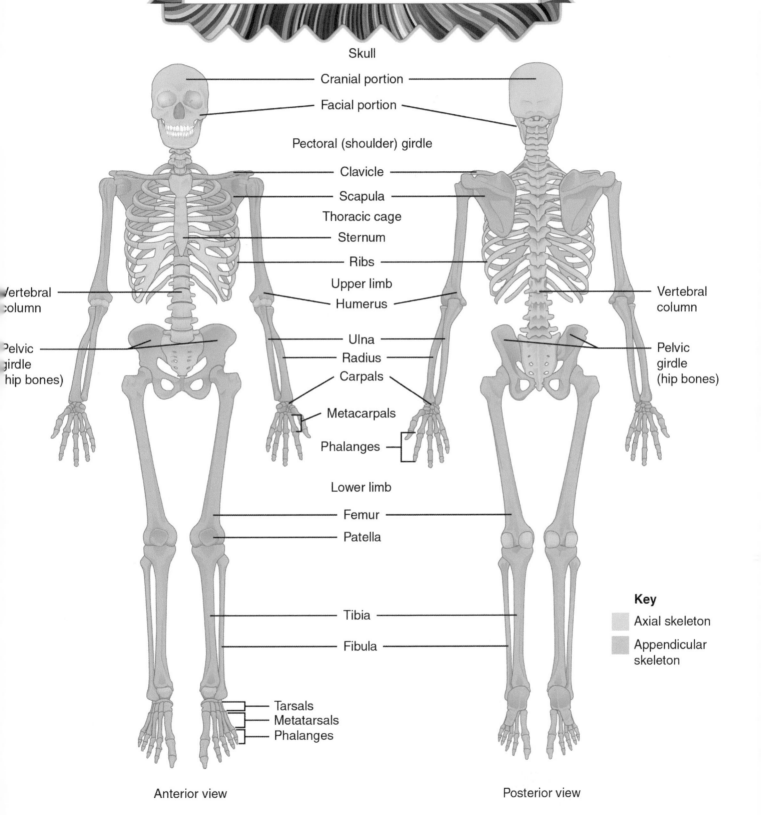

Skull

Cranial portion

Facial portion

Pectoral (shoulder) girdle

Clavicle

Scapula

Thoracic cage

Sternum

Ribs

Upper limb

Humerus

Ulna

Radius

Carpals

Metacarpals

Phalanges

Lower limb

Femur

Patella

Tibia

Fibula

Tarsals

Metatarsals

Phalanges

Vertebral column

Pelvic girdle (hip bones)

Vertebral column

Pelvic girdle (hip bones)

Key

Axial skeleton

Appendicular skeleton

Anterior view

Posterior view

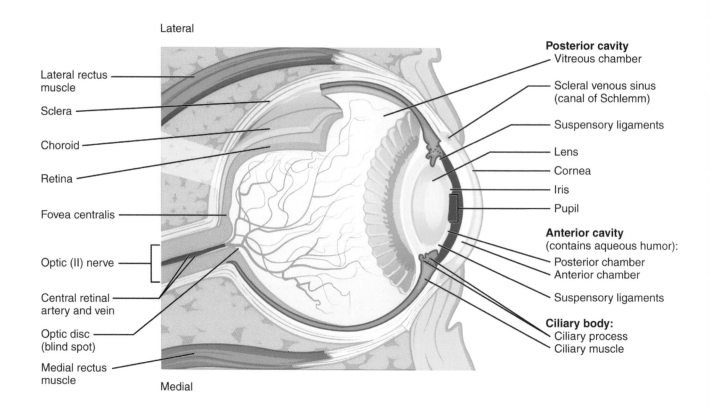

Lateral

Lateral rectus muscle

Sclera

Choroid

Retina

Fovea centralis

Optic (II) nerve

Central retinal artery and vein

Optic disc (blind spot)

Medial rectus muscle

Medial

Posterior cavity
Vitreous chamber

Scleral venous sinus (canal of Schlemm)

Suspensory ligaments

Lens

Cornea

Iris

Pupil

Anterior cavity (contains aqueous humor):
Posterior chamber
Anterior chamber

Suspensory ligaments

Ciliary body:
Ciliary process
Ciliary muscle

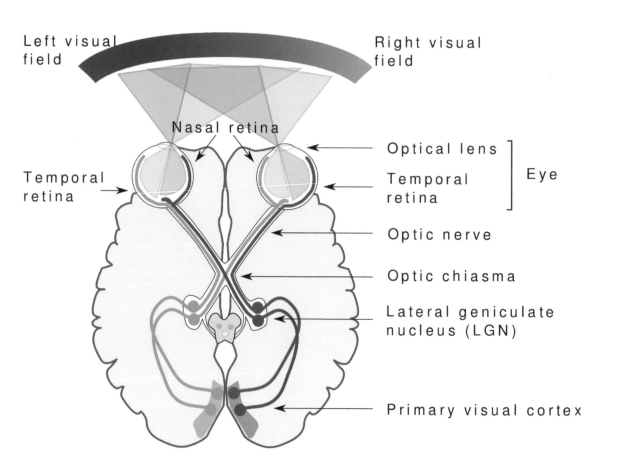

Left visual field

Right visual field

Nasal retina

Temporal retina

Optical lens

Temporal retina

Eye

Optic nerve

Optic chiasma

Lateral geniculate nucleus (LGN)

Primary visual cortex

Eye and vision anatomy

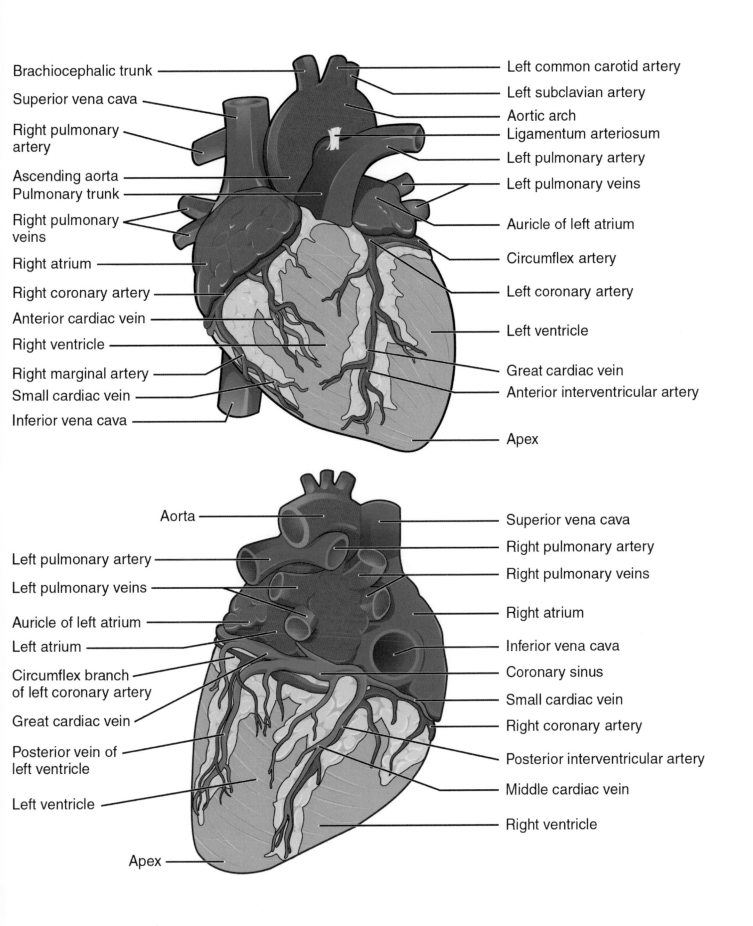

Brachiocephalic trunk

Superior vena cava

Right pulmonary artery

Ascending aorta

Pulmonary trunk

Right pulmonary veins

Right atrium

Right coronary artery

Anterior cardiac vein

Right ventricle

Right marginal artery

Small cardiac vein

Inferior vena cava

Left common carotid artery

Left subclavian artery

Aortic arch

Ligamentum arteriosum

Left pulmonary artery

Left pulmonary veins

Auricle of left atrium

Circumflex artery

Left coronary artery

Left ventricle

Great cardiac vein

Anterior interventricular artery

Apex

Aorta

Left pulmonary artery

Left pulmonary veins

Auricle of left atrium

Left atrium

Circumflex branch of left coronary artery

Great cardiac vein

Posterior vein of left ventricle

Left ventricle

Apex

Superior vena cava

Right pulmonary artery

Right pulmonary veins

Right atrium

Inferior vena cava

Coronary sinus

Small cardiac vein

Right coronary artery

Posterior interventricular artery

Middle cardiac vein

Right ventricle

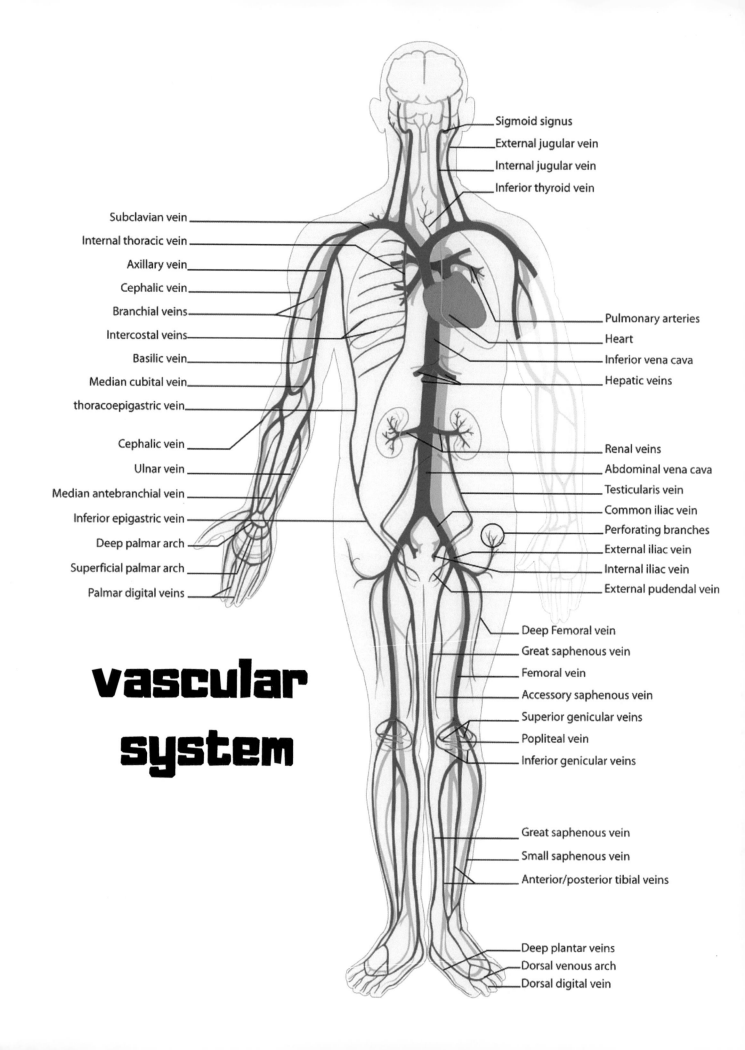

Sigmoid signus
External jugular vein
Internal jugular vein
Inferior thyroid vein

Subclavian vein
Internal thoracic vein
Axillary vein
Cephalic vein
Branchial veins
Intercostal veins
Basilic vein
Median cubital vein
thoracoepigastric vein

Cephalic vein
Ulnar vein
Median antebranchial vein
Inferior epigastric vein
Deep palmar arch
Superficial palmar arch
Palmar digital veins

Pulmonary arteries
Heart
Inferior vena cava
Hepatic veins

Renal veins
Abdominal vena cava
Testicularis vein
Common iliac vein
Perforating branches
External iliac vein
Internal iliac vein
External pudendal vein

Deep Femoral vein
Great saphenous vein
Femoral vein
Accessory saphenous vein
Superior genicular veins
Popliteal vein
Inferior genicular veins

Great saphenous vein
Small saphenous vein
Anterior/posterior tibial veins

Deep plantar veins
Dorsal venous arch
Dorsal digital vein

vascular
system

Muscles and Innervation

Anterior View

- Sternocleidomastoid
- Deltoid
- Pectoralis major
- Rectus abdominis
- Abdominal external oblique
- Pectineus
- Adductor longus
- Sartorius
- Rectus femoris
- Vastus lateralis
- Fibularis longus
- Tibialis anterior

- Occipitofrontalis (frontal belly)
- Trapezius
- Pectoralis minor
- Serratus anterior
- Biceps brachii
- Brachialis
- Brachioradialis
- Pronator teres
- Flexor carpi radialis
- Tensor fasciae latae
- Iliopsoas
- Gracilis
- Vastus medialis
- Soleus and gastrocnemius

Major muscles of the body.
Right side: superficial; left side:
deep (anterior view)

Posterior View

- Occipitofrontalis (occipital belly)
- Splenius capitis
- Levator scapulae
- Supraspinatus
- Teres minor
- Infraspinatus
- Teres major
- Triceps brachii
- Serratus posterior inferior
- External oblique
- Gluteus medius (dissected)
- Gluteus maximus (dissected)
- Semimembranosus
- Peroneus longus
- Tibialis posterior

- Epicranial aponeurosis
- Rhomboids
- Trapezius
- Deltoid
- Latissimus dorsi
- Brachioradialis
- Extensor carpi radialis
- Extensor digitorum
- Extensor carpi ulnaris
- Flexor carpi ulnaris
- Gluteus minimus
- Gemellus muscles
- Biceps femoris
- Semitendinosus
- Gracilis
- Gastrocnemius (dissected)
- Soleus

Major muscles of the body.
Right side: superficial; left side:
deep (posterior view)

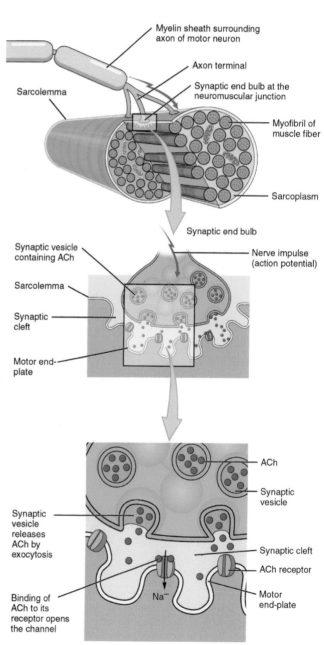

- Myelin sheath surrounding axon of motor neuron
- Axon terminal
- Synaptic end bulb at the neuromuscular junction
- Sarcolemma
- Myofibril of muscle fiber
- Sarcoplasm

- Synaptic end bulb
- Synaptic vesicle containing ACh
- Nerve impulse (action potential)
- Sarcolemma
- Synaptic cleft
- Motor end-plate

- ACh
- Synaptic vesicle
- Synaptic vesicle releases ACh by exocytosis
- Synaptic cleft
- ACh receptor
- Motor end-plate
- Binding of ACh to its receptor opens the channel
- Na$^-$

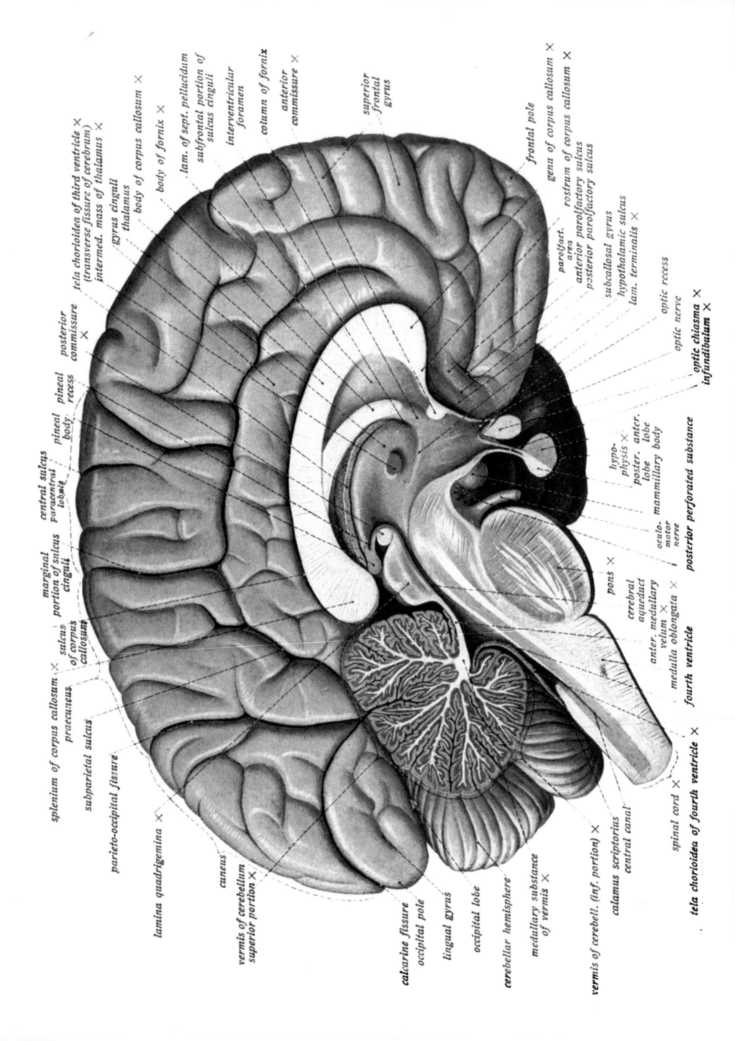

Printed in Great Britain
by Amazon

58347379R00017